UNCOVERING HISTORY

THE BIBLE LANDS

First published by McRae Books
Copyright © 2005 McRae Books Srl, Florence (Italy)
Borgo Santa Croce, 8 – 50122 – Florence (Italy)
This edition published under license from McRae Books. All rights
reserved.

SERIES EDITOR Anne McRae
TEXT Cath Senker
CONSULTANT Revd. Dr. Steve Motyer
ILLUSTRATIONS MM comunicazione (Manuela Cappon, Monica Favilli) ps.
32–33, 40–41; Giacinto Gaudenzi ps. 10–11, 19, 30–31; Lucia Mattioli ps.
26–27; Alessandro Menchi p. 37; Leonardo Meschini ps. 34–35, 36;
Francesca D'Ottavi p. 42–43; Paola Ravaglia ps. 20–21, 39, 45; Claudia
Saraceni ps. 8–9, 12, 13, 14–15, 16–17, 24–25; Sergio ps. 22–23, 28–29
ILLUSTRATIONS Lucia Mattioli, Francesca D'Ottavi, Studio Stalio (Alessandro
Cantucci, Fabiano Fabbrucci, Margherita Salvadori)
MAPS Paola Baldanzi
GRAPHIC DESIGN Marco Nardi
LAYOUT Rebecca Milner
PROJECT EDITOR Claire Moore
REPRO Litocolor, Florence

Published in the United States by Smart Apple Media
2140 Howard Drive West, North Mankato, Minnesota 56003

U.S. publication copyright © 2006 Smart Apple Media
International copyright reserved in all countries. No part of this book
may be reproduced in any form without written permission from the
publisher.
Printed and bound in Belgium

Library of Congress Cataloging-in-Publication Data

Senker, Cath.
Everyday life in the Bible lands / by Cath Senker.
p. cm. — (Uncovering history)
Includes index.
ISBN 1-58340-711-1
1. Bible—History of biblical events—Juvenile literature. I. Title. II. Series.

BS635.3.S46 2005
220.9'5—dc22   2004059034

9 8 7 6 5 4 3 2 1

UNCOVERING HISTORY

Cath Senker

EVERYDAY LIFE IN THE

BIBLE LANDS

Illustrations by MM comunicazione, Giacinto Gaudenzi, Lucia Mattioli, Alessandro Menchi, Leonardo Meschini, Francesca D'Ottavi, Paola Ravaglia, Claudia Saraceni, Sergio, Studio Stalio

A⁺
Smart Apple Media

Table of Contents

Introduction

The Bible Lands have a long and complex history. Including present-day Lebanon, Syria, Israel, and Jordan, people have lived in the Bible Lands since the earliest prehistoric times. Over the centuries that followed, the Bible Lands were settled and conquered by many different peoples and witnessed the development of a unique culture and civilization.

The first towns and cities started to appear around 3000 B.C., and the ancient Israelites probably settled in the Bible Lands between 2000 and 1750 B.C. Extensive trade networks were quickly established between East and West. When the first forms of writing appeared in Canaan around 1500 B.C., they greatly facilitated commerce and social organization. Around 1000 B.C., the united monarchy of Israel and Judah was established, and the magnificent Jewish Temple was built in Jerusalem. Coming under Greek rule in 332 B.C. and then Roman rule in 63 B.C., the Bible Lands where Jesus lived and preached were very different from those where King Solomon's people had lived.

Perhaps the most reliable source of information on life in the Bible Lands is the Bible itself. Both the Old and New Testaments provide us with fairly detailed snapshots of the everyday lives of people at this time. In this book, we learn about the world in which people lived—their homes, entertainment, religious celebrations, education, food, and clothing, not to mention the problems caused by war and invasion.

Chronology of the Bible Lands

THE PEOPLES OF THE BIBLE LANDS BEGIN TO CULTIVATE CROPS
8000–6000 B.C.

THE INVENTION OF POTTERY
6000 B.C.

THE BEGINNING OF METALWORKING
c. 4500 B.C.

THE DEVELOPMENT OF TOWNS AND CITIES IN PALESTINE
3000 B.C.

FIRST WRITING SYSTEM SPREADS TO THE BIBLE LANDS
3000–1600 B.C.

THE TIME OF THE PATRIARCHS
c. 2000–1750 B.C.

THE BIBLE IS WRITTEN
1000 B.C.–A.D. 100

KING DAVID ESTABLISHES THE UNITED KINGDOM OF ISRAEL
c. 1000 B.C.

KING SOLOMON'S TEMPLE IS BUILT
c. 960 B.C.

THE ASSYRIANS SEIZE THE KINGDOM OF ISRAEL
722 B.C.

THE DESTRUCTION OF THE FIRST JEWISH TEMPLE IN JERUSALEM
586 B.C.

JEWS ARE PERMITTED TO RETURN TO JERUSALEM
538 B.C.

ALEXANDER THE GREAT CONQUERS PALESTINE FOR THE GREEKS
332 B.C.

PALESTINE COMES UNDER THE RULE OF PROCURATORS RESPONSIBLE TO ROME
63 B.C.

KING HEROD REIGNS AS KING OF JUDAEA
37–4 B.C.

APPROXIMATE DATE OF JESUS'S BIRTH
6–4 B.C.

THE DESTRUCTION OF THE SECOND JEWISH TEMPLE
A.D. 70

CHRISTIANITY BECOMES THE OFFICIAL RELIGION OF THE BYZANTINE EMPIRE
392

Natufian culture

The Natufians were the first people to live in permanent villages. The large number of burials inside their settlement areas testifies to their sedentary lifestyle. Their homes were partly dug into the ground and covered with animal hides or branches. They lived by hunting gazelle, fallow deer, and wild boar, trapping birds, and gathering plants.

The Natufians produced some art objects and jewelry, including body decorations and stone figurines. This necklace (above) is made of shell, eggs, bone, and stone.

MEDITERRANEAN SEA

Yabrud III

Eynan (Ain Mallaha)

Nahal Ein Gev II

Sefunim
Nahal Oren
El-Wad
Kebara
Rakefet

Jericho

Umm ez-Zuweitina

Beidha

Above: A map showing early Natufian settlements in the Bible Lands. Natufian culture dates from 10,800 to 8500 B.C.

Natufian settlements were often located close to springs or rivers. This illustration shows a group of Natufians at Ain Mallaha in northern Israel. While hunting and fishing were important means of survival for the Natufians, evidence also shows that they harvested grain.

Before the Bible

The Bible Lands have been inhabited since the earliest prehistoric times. Remains of both Neanderthals and *Homo Sapiens*, the first modern humans, have been discovered in many areas. Between 8000 and 6000 B.C., some peoples of the Middle East began to grow their own crops instead of hunting and gathering food. This gradual transition to life in farming communities is known as the Neolithic Revolution.

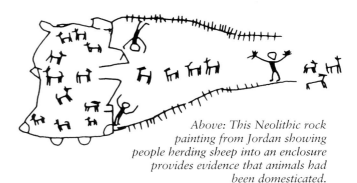

Above: This Neolithic rock painting from Jordan showing people herding sheep into an enclosure provides evidence that animals had been domesticated.

Traces of prehistory

Early humans first founded populations in the Middle East around 1.5 million years ago. Archaeological discoveries include pebble-tools—crude pebbles with cutting edges—and flint hand-axes. In the caves at Mount Carmel, in present-day Israel, the discovery of skeletal remains and tools indicate that both Neanderthals and early modern humans lived in the region. In Kebara Cave, also in Israel, Neanderthal skeletons have been found.

This partial Neanderthal skeleton was found at Kebara Cave, Israel, in 1983.

The Neolithic Revolution

Around 8000 B.C., the Natufians began to cultivate wheat and barley for food. They also started to domesticate animals, including sheep and goats, to provide milk, meat, wool, and hides. It was a transformation that took thousands of years but enabled people to settle permanently in one place instead of roaming to find food.

This cornet-shaped cup from around 3500 B.C. was found in the Jordan Valley. It might have been a drinking cup.

The first cities

Around 3000 B.C., towns and cities developed in Palestine. The towns were generally built on major trade routes. These towns required sophisticated social organization in order to construct fortified walls, temples, and administration buildings. At Megiddo (see pages 40–41), the houses may have been arranged in a grid pattern, and at Arad and Ai, there were large artificial reservoirs to hold the winter rain.

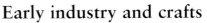

Above: This reconstruction shows the city of Jericho.

This copper scepter-head (right) with two ibexes was found in the Judaean Desert. It is part of a scepter, a ceremonial object.

Early industry and crafts

Along with the establishment of agriculture came the development of industry and crafts. In about 6000 B.C., pottery was invented. At first, it was very crude and probably fired in domestic hearths at a low temperature. Around 4500 B.C., however, a huge technological leap marked the beginning of metalworking, mostly using copper.

This small figure dates from around 6800 B.C. and probably represents a sacred god or spirit.

Family caravans were a common sight in the early Bible Lands. Semi-nomads often traveled between towns and cities in search of work. At about 17-mile (27-km) intervals, there were small settlements where travelers could stop and rest.

Right: Canaanite pottery from the period of the Patriarchs.

Below: This map shows Abraham's journey from Ur to Canaan.

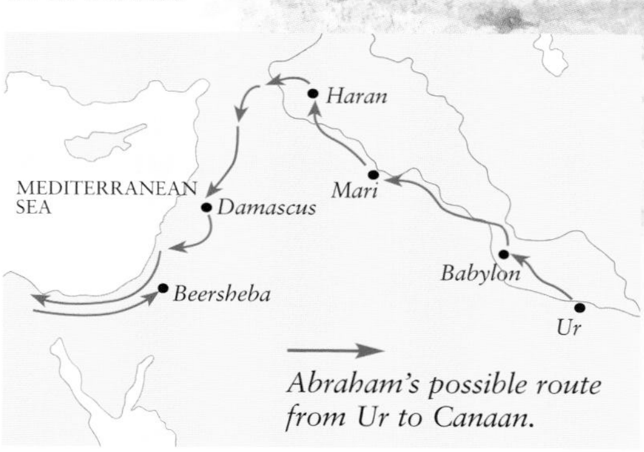

Haran

MEDITERRANEAN SEA

Damascus   Mari

Babylon

Beersheba

Ur

Abraham's possible route from Ur to Canaan.

Who were the Patriarchs?

The word "patriarch" means "male leader" or "father" of a family or people. The first Patriarch of the people of Israel was Abraham. Upon his death, leadership passed to his son Isaac, and subsequently to Isaac's son Jacob. Jacob had 12 sons, all of whom were considered to be Patriarchs. According to the Bible, the 12 tribes of Israel were descended from Jacob's sons.

The Time of the Patriarchs

In the Bible, the Patriarchs were the ancestors of the 12 tribes of Israel: Abraham, Isaac, Jacob, and Joseph. It is hard to prove whether they actually existed, and if they did, exactly when they lived. Most scholars believe that the patriarchal stories are set in 2000 to 1750 B.C. At that time, there were many powerful cities in the Middle East, linked by trade routes. According to the Bible, Abraham and his family migrated from Ur in Mesopotamia to the land of Canaan, the name for an area centered in Palestine.

A section of stained glass window showing Abraham, the founding father of Israel in the Bible.

Above: A Canaanite gold star pendant from the 16th century B.C.

Canaan culture

During the age of the Patriarchs, cities expanded in Canaan; the most important were Carchemish, Qatna, and Hazor. The Canaanites were known for their skill in metalwork, particularly jewelry and ivory carving. It is possible that between 2000 and 1600 B.C., the Canaanites first developed the alphabetic system of writing, which was later perfected by the Phoenicians (see pages 26–27).

This man, probably a Canaanite, and his donkey are from an Egyptian wall-painting dating from 1900 B.C. They are perhaps traveling to trade or to settle.

On the move

It was common for families to migrate. The Bible describes how Abraham, his wife, father, and nephew left Ur, accompanied by their servants, sheep, and cattle. They traveled to Haran and then headed west. On the way to Canaan, they passed through Aleppo, Qatna, Damascus, and Hazor, resting at settlements between the towns. There is no archaeological proof of the journey, but such a trip was feasible.

Traveling to trade

An extensive trading network among the cities of the Middle East existed between 2000 and 1000 B.C. A road linked Egypt and Palestine, and there were sea routes to the Palestinian coastal cities. Goods from Arabia and Africa arrived at the ports, and caravans transported goods overland. Essential items such as copper and oil were traded, as well as luxury goods such as gold, silver, and textiles. There were frequent wars among large cities to gain control over profitable international trade routes.

A relief stone showing a loaded pack camel being led through the desert.

Food and Agriculture

The development of agriculture was a significant advance for the people of the Bible Lands, enabling them to settle in one place and produce the food they needed. Over time, they selected plants that were suitable for cultivation and learned to domesticate animals. Farmers usually relied on the winter rains to water their crops, but occasionally the land was hit by drought. Disease and pests could also mean disaster for farmers, wiping out crops and animals.

This Mesopotamian stone carving from about 860 B.C. shows different scenes in the preparation of a king's meal.

Left: Figs grew in many parts of the Bible Lands.

Right: Grain was winnowed (fanned in the wind with a fork) to separate the heavy grains from the chaff.

Both men and women gathered wheat during the harvest season.

Below: An olive press. The top stone (which would have had a handle) was used to crush the olives, and the oil flowed out below.

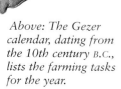

Above: The Gezer calendar, dating from the 10th century B.C., lists the farming tasks for the year.

Working the land

Early economy was based on agriculture. The farmer's year began with clearing the rocky land and terracing hillsides. The land was plowed using a team of oxen or mules. Farmers sowed the seeds by hand and sometimes fertilized their fields with manure. Later, they harvested their crops with hand-held sickles.

Women usually made and baked bread. The family's oven was just outside the house and was usually made from clay and lined with stones.

Daily bread

Most meals consisted of bread eaten with a variety of vegetables that were boiled with herbs to give flavor. Bread was the staple food; round, flat loaves were made from wheat or barley. For most people, meat was a rare luxury. People who lived near the sea caught fish, which was eaten fresh or dried and salted for storing. Cooking methods were simple; most food was boiled in a pot over a wood fire.

Sheep were extremely useful, providing meat, fat, milk, wool, and skins for producing clothing.

Above: A butcher in Jerusalem. Only wealthy people could afford to eat meat.

Dietary laws

The Israelites followed the dietary laws of the Jewish tradition. They could not eat meat that still retained blood and were prohibited from eating pigs, camels, and rabbits. They were, however, permitted to eat some animals, such as deer, goats, and sheep. Meat and dairy products were never consumed during the same meal.

Women usually filled clay water pitchers like this one (right) with water at the well or underground reservoir.

Crops and animals

The main crops grown by the Israelites were wheat, barley, grapes, figs, olives, pomegranates, and dates. The Bible describes many animals kept for their milk and meat, including sheep, goats, cattle, and pigs—however, the Israelites were forbidden to eat the latter. Other animals, such as donkeys, horses, and camels, were domesticated for pulling loads and used as beasts of burden. Chickens were also kept for their eggs and meat.

Water and wine

Water was a vital resource for drinking, farming, and purification for religious ceremonies. The Israelites depended mainly on rainfall and springs for water. They also dug wells and learned to build underground water tunnels (see pages 15 and 34). The climate was suitable for growing grapevines, and wine was often drunk at meals.

A lively street scene in a Bible Lands town.

There were no specially constructed shops in biblical towns. Traders like this fruit vendor (right) set out their goods on a stall at the side of the street or on the ground. This trader is using an umbrella to protect herself and her goods from the strong sun.

Streets and shopping

The market was the hub of the town, where craftworkers such as weavers, potters, and carpenters produced and sold their wares. Traders sold food and other goods from small stalls. Towns had no running water, garbage collection, or sewage system; water came from public wells, and there were open gutters that allowed diseases to spread easily. Rich people usually lived in fine houses in a separate part of the town.

Town Life

Towns and villages existed in the Bible Lands long before patriarchal times. Settlements ranged from tiny, unwalled villages to well-defended cities with fortifications to deter invaders. Towns were often located at the junction of trade routes. Although not as strongly fortified as cities, they had walls and gates. Villagers from neighboring areas often fled to them for protection in times of war.

This plan of the town of Marisa, near Jerusalem, shows that the streets followed an orderly design.

Town planning

Israelite towns and cities began to show well-developed town planning from about 1000 B.C. In the major administrative center of Megiddo in the late 10th century B.C., four-fifths of the city's land was taken up by public structures. In the less important city of Beersheba, however, public structures were integrated into the city rather than confined to a specific quarter.

Well-watered

It was vital for each town to have a good water supply, both to ensure supplies during the parched summer months and to quench the townspeople's thirst during sieges. Megiddo had a hidden tunnel built below the city that led to a spring. In Beersheba, stairs were cut into the ground, leading down to a water supply.

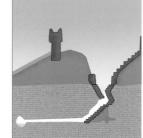

Above: This diagram shows the water tunnel in Megiddo. The spring provided a reliable source of clean water.

Most towns built a simple synagogue like this (right).

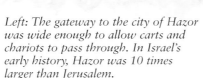

Left: The gateway to the city of Hazor was wide enough to allow carts and chariots to pass through. In Israel's early history, Hazor was 10 times larger than Jerusalem.

Wall-to-wall security

During the time of the Israelite kings Saul, David, and Solomon (around 1000 B.C.), many towns had strong walls, gates, and sometimes towers. Gateways were built of stone and had guard chambers in them. The gate was a wooden double door, sometimes covered with metal. At night, the city gates were firmly closed and locked with heavy beams.

Important buildings

The most important buildings in a town were usually linked to government or religion. In the ninth century B.C., Samaria had a large complex including storerooms, the royal palace, and administrative buildings. In Jerusalem, King Solomon (ruled c. 965–926 B.C.) built an impressive stone temple (see pages 24–25).

Houses and Homes

Homes in biblical times were often used as a workplace as well as a place to eat and sleep. They varied greatly, from nomads' goatskin tents to strongly built stone houses. For ordinary people, the home was uncomfortably hot in summer, and filled with smoke from the fire in winter. The roof and walls often leaked when it rained. From Solomon's time, wealthy people lived in homes with many rooms, which often had shaded courtyards and gardens.

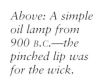

Above: A simple oil lamp from 900 B.C.—the pinched lip was for the wick.

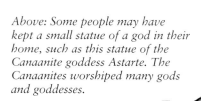

Above: Some people may have kept a small statue of a god in their home, such as this statue of the Canaanite goddess Astarte. The Canaanites worshiped many gods and goddesses.

Important buildings, such as palaces and large houses, could be locked using a key like this one from Roman times (left), probably made from wood.

An Israelite home

Most homes were very small. A whole family often lived in one single room, perhaps with a mud-brick partition in the middle. Around the early 15th century B.C., four-room houses were constructed. Around the central courtyard, there were one or two storage rooms, a living room, and a bedroom— sometimes the rooms were subdivided. An outside staircase or ladder led to the roof. Wealthy homes had more rooms, and some had two floors.

Inside the house

Poor people had little furniture. The entire family often slept on a thin, wool mattress under goat's-hair quilts and ate from a straw mat on the floor. All homes had storage jars for flour and oil, jars for fetching and storing water, and cooking pots. An oil lamp was essential, as rooms were dark. Wealthy people usually had beds, tables, and chairs, and after about 300 B.C., a few had mosaic floors in the Greek style.

A bronze jug and wooden-handled iron knife from the first century A.D.

Above: A scene in an Assyrian camp—an armed officer enters a large tent. Soldiers slept in tents while traveling on military campaigns.

Mobile homes

In the Bible Lands, there were many nomads who carried their tent homes with them. A tent was made by propping up a length of goat's-hair cloth and tying it to poles with ropes. The back was closed in with a goat's-hair screen. The tent was divided into two rooms with a curtain in the middle—the open, front part was for receiving visitors, while the back section was occupied by the women and used for storage.

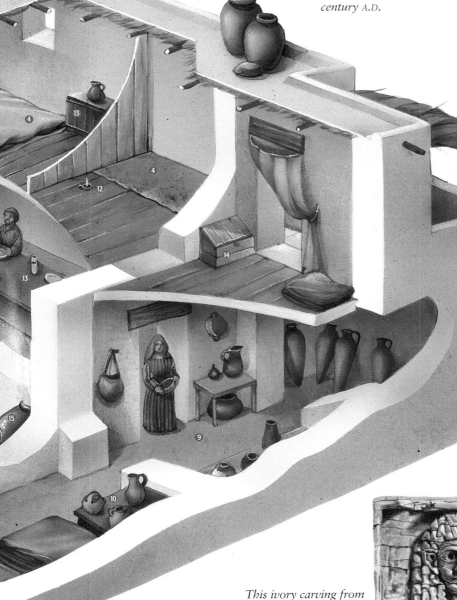

A stone house belonging to an Israelite family.

This ivory carving from Nimrud, capital of the Assyrian Empire, shows a woman looking out a window, which was simply a hole in the wall.

❶ FLAT ROOF OFTEN USED TO STORE ANIMAL FOOD OR DRY CROPS
❷ DRIED MUD-BRICK WALLS
❸ MAIN LIVING AREA
❹ SLEEPING MAT
❺ THE ROOMS WERE BUILT AROUND A CENTRAL COURTYARD
❻ THE FLOOR WAS MADE OF BEATEN MUD
❼ SPACE FOR ANIMALS
❽ NO GLASS IN THE WINDOWS
❾ STOREROOM, WHERE GRAIN AND OTHER GOODS WERE STORED IN COOL, DRY CONDITIONS
❿ WATER AND WINE JUGS
⓫ GOATSKIN BAG FOR CARRYING WATER
⓬ EARTHENWARE LAMP
⓭ SIMPLE FURNITURE
⓮ TRUNK FOR STORING PRECIOUS ITEMS
⓯ OVENS WHERE BREAD WAS BAKED

People and Cultures

A wide range of people with different cultures lived in the Bible Lands. The civilizations of Ancient Egypt, Babylonia, and Assyria all influenced the region through conquest, trade, and cultural exchange. Several smaller nations also existed, including the Arameans, Ammonites, and Edomites. Conflict frequently erupted between the different peoples as they vied for control of territory and trade. At other times, however, they lived peacefully side by side.

Above: Pottery created by the Philistines. Belonging to the Mycenaean-type made in Greece and Crete, it indicates that the Philistines originally came from this region.

This illustration shows how the Israelites would have traveled to Canaan—on foot, accompanied by mules loaded with their possessions.

The Philistines

The Philistines were one of the Sea Peoples that began to arrive in the eastern Mediterranean around the 14th century B.C. They settled in southern Canaan, living in five city-states—Ashdod, Ashkelon, and Gaza on the coast, and Gath and Ekron inland. In the 11th century B.C., they attempted to expand their territory eastward, which brought them into conflict with the Israelites.

The Israelites unite

In the 13th century B.C., the Israelites were enslaved by the pharaohs in Egypt. According to the biblical story in Exodus, Moses led them out of Egypt and into Canaan. The Israelites settled easily into farming life, but in the 11th century B.C., they came into conflict with the Philistines. The Israelites united into one kingdom for defense, and under King David (reigned c. 1000–962 B.C.), they defeated the Philistines.

Knowing the neighbors

Powerful and influential civilizations adjoined the Bible Lands. The Egyptians brought Canaan under their control around 1550 B.C. They imposed heavy taxes, but in return the Canaanite cities benefited from improved access to international trade. From 3000 to 1600 B.C., the first writing system spread to the Bible Lands from Babylonia, along with knowledge of astronomy and mathematics.

Right: The siege and capture of Lachish in 701 B.C. are illustrated in a series of relief carvings from Assyrian king Sennacherib's palace.

Left: Ramesses the Great (reigned 1279–13 B.C.), a powerful pharaoh. Under his rule, some Canaanite cities were strengthened, such as Beth Shan and Gaza, while others fell into decline.

Waging war

From the ninth century B.C., Assyria fought to expand its territory, launching regular military campaigns against Syria, Phoenicia, Israel, and Judah. The Assyrians seized the northern kingdom of Israel in 722 B.C., and later attacked the southern kingdom of Judah. In 701 B.C., they destroyed many cities, including Lachish. In turn, the Babylonians, under King Nabopolassar, defeated the Assyrians in 612 B.C. and claimed their lands.

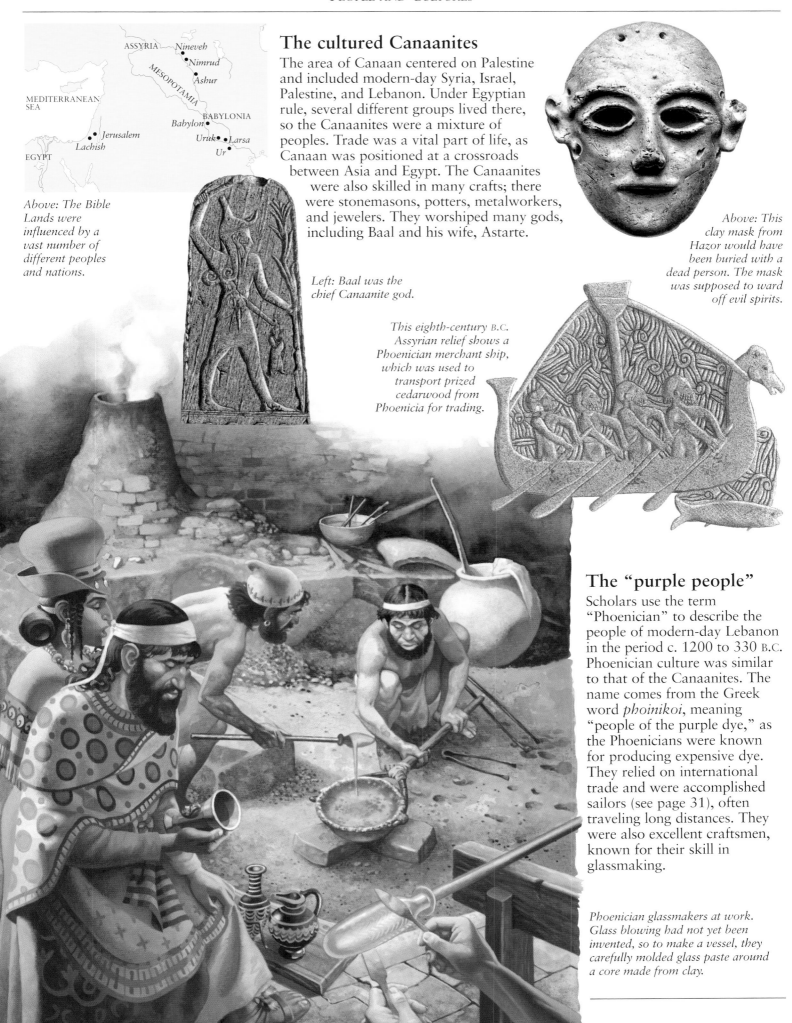

Above: The Bible Lands were influenced by a vast number of different peoples and nations.

The cultured Canaanites

The area of Canaan centered on Palestine and included modern-day Syria, Israel, Palestine, and Lebanon. Under Egyptian rule, several different groups lived there, so the Canaanites were a mixture of peoples. Trade was a vital part of life, as Canaan was positioned at a crossroads between Asia and Egypt. The Canaanites were also skilled in many crafts; there were stonemasons, potters, metalworkers, and jewelers. They worshiped many gods, including Baal and his wife, Astarte.

Left: Baal was the chief Canaanite god.

This eighth-century B.C. Assyrian relief shows a Phoenician merchant ship, which was used to transport prized cedarwood from Phoenicia for trading.

Above: This clay mask from Hazor would have been buried with a dead person. The mask was supposed to ward off evil spirits.

The "purple people"

Scholars use the term "Phoenician" to describe the people of modern-day Lebanon in the period c. 1200 to 330 B.C. Phoenician culture was similar to that of the Canaanites. The name comes from the Greek word *phoinikoi*, meaning "people of the purple dye," as the Phoenicians were known for producing expensive dye. They relied on international trade and were accomplished sailors (see page 31), often traveling long distances. They were also excellent craftsmen, known for their skill in glassmaking.

Phoenician glassmakers at work. Glass blowing had not yet been invented, so to make a vessel, they carefully molded glass paste around a core made from clay.

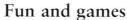

Fun and games

The Bible does not refer to toys, but archaeological evidence proves they existed. Findings include clay figurines that could have been dolls, dolls' houses, or wooden pull-along toys on wheels. Miniature cooking pots and furniture made from pottery have also been discovered. Board games such as chess and draughts were extremely popular, as were solitaire and a form of ludo. Knucklebones was a game that used the dried ankle bones of sheep.

Above: Two girls playing knucklebones; the player tossed them in the air and scored points depending on which side the bones landed.

Left: These Roman dice were used for board games. Dice games were popular, but Jewish religious leaders disapproved of gambling.

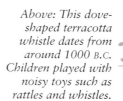

Above: This dove-shaped terracotta whistle dates from around 1000 B.C. Children played with noisy toys such as rattles and whistles.

Festivals and feasting

The Jewish calendar included festivals celebrating the main phases of the agricultural year and significant events in Jewish history. Passover was a commemoration of the Exodus from slavery in Egypt (see page 18), during which the Israelites ate ceremonial foods. Shavuot was a harvest celebration at which the best-quality first fruits were offered in the Temple. At Sukkot (see pages 22–23), there was a week-long festival to remember the Jewish people's wanderings in the desert after their escape from Egypt.

On some Jewish holidays, there were feasts, when families would gather for a festive meal.

Sports

Some sports, such as running races, wrestling, and archery, existed in Old Testament times. Other sports were brought to the Holy Land by the Seleucid Greeks in the fourth century B.C. The Greeks enjoyed exercise; they practiced running, boxing, wrestling, discus and javelin throwing, and chariot racing. Some Jewish people, however, opposed such activities because of their link with Greek pagan traditions; they also objected to the contestants competing naked.

Left: This Greek marble relief from the sixth century B.C. shows two men wrestling.

In Old Testament times, it is probable that women were the main music makers. Music was often played to celebrate a military victory or to welcome soldiers home.

Lively music

The Old Testament mentions the use of music in worship—for example, cymbals were played. By New Testament times, music was a regular feature in people's lives. Feasts and festivals were always accompanied by music. The kinnor was a lyre, or harp, and the khalil was a double-reed instrument. Largely played by women, the tambourine accompanied processions, dances, and feasts. Some Jewish children learned to play musical instruments as part of their education.

Entertainment

Most people in biblical times had a hard working life. For Jewish people, however, every sabbath was a day of rest. There were also many religious festivals to break the monotonous cycle of daily life, in which music played an important role. Music and dancing were popular forms of entertainment; stringed, wind, and percussion instruments were played. There were also various kinds of board games, and sporting activities such as racing and wrestling. Children had their own entertainments; archaeologists have discovered elaborate toys such as dolls' houses.

This terracotta figure of a woman playing a drum, dating from the ninth or eighth century B.C., was found on the Carmel coast of Israel.

A kinnor was a small harp, or lyre, with a wooden frame. It is mentioned in the Mishna, the code of Jewish law, that the entrails of birds were used to make the strings.

A suitable match

Marriage was the foundation of Israelite society. Fathers made the match between two young people, choosing a partner from the extended family. By New Testament times, the minimum age for marriage was fixed at 12 for girls and 13 for boys. The bridegroom's father paid a bride price to the girl's father, who in return provided a dowry. At the wedding, there was a lavish banquet and a procession through the streets with singing and dancing.

Above: Babylonian figures of a married couple. In Israelite society, polygamy was acceptable—a man could marry two or more wives as long as he could provide for them.

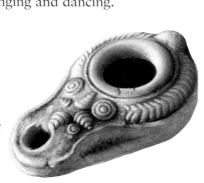

If the wedding procession was in the evening, the bride's attendants carried earthenware oil lamps like this (right) to light the way.

Customs and Rituals

The family formed a strong unit in biblical times. Family members lived near each other, and children learned skills from their parents and worked with the family from a young age. Israelite boys became adults in the legal and religious sense when they were 13. Most were married by their late teens to even younger girls. The important stages of life were all marked with special ceremonies, from birth to marriage and death.

The circumcision ceremony

When an Israelite baby boy was eight days old, he was circumcized by his father (the foreskin of his penis was removed with a knife). Most neighboring peoples also practiced circumcision, but the Israelites saw the rite as a symbol of their special relationship with God and as a symbol of purity.

Arrival in the world

There was a high mortality rate for babies, and children therefore were highly valued. Babies' names were carefully chosen by the father or mother; the name might refer to events at the time, the circumstances of birth, or to God himself. The newborn baby was washed and rubbed with salt and then wrapped in swaddling clothes to keep the limbs close to its sides. The clothes were loosened several times a day and the skin rubbed with olive oil. A mother usually breastfed her infant for up to three years.

This medieval miniature shows a father holding a knife, about to circumcize a baby boy who sits in the arms of a relative.

Left: This figurine of a pregnant woman, which was found in a cemetery in the Phoenician city-port of Achziv, dates from the sixth century B.C.

These villagers are preparing for Sukkot, by building small huts, with three sides and a roof made from palm branches and other greenery, on the roof of their house. They will eat and sleep in the hut during the holiday.

There was a limited number of caves available for burying bodies, so the bones of the dead were often removed and placed in chests called ossuaries, like this earthenware example (right).

Religious festivals

The calendar was punctuated with religious festivals, including Passover, Sukkot, and Yom Kippur. At Passover, families ate only unleavened bread known as matzah, as their forefathers had done during their escape from Egypt. At Sukkot, the Israelites stayed in temporary huts for a week to remember the shelters in which their forefathers had slept. At Yom Kippur, they prayed to God to forgive them for their sins.

Above: Matzah—flat, unleavened bread. When the Israelites fled Egypt, they had no time to bake bread. Instead, they carried raw dough with them, which hardened into flat crackers.

Mourning the dead

When a person died in biblical times, the body was buried quickly. At the funeral, people expressed their grief openly by crying and tearing their clothes. Following the burial, there was a mourning period of seven days, during which neighbors visited the family with food. Most people were buried in the open ground or in caves, but rich people had burial chambers cut into rock. Elaborate graves with jewelry, pottery, food, and drink have also been discovered.

This bracelet was found in a child's grave excavated in modern-day Jordan. The child must have come from a wealthy family because the bracelet includes silver beads.

Religion

The Israelite religion—Judaism—began when Abraham led his people from Egypt to Canaan. It was the first monotheistic religion, stressing the existence of one God alone. Other peoples in the Bible Lands worshiped a variety of gods and goddesses, often related to natural phenomena such as the moon and sun, or fertility and the harvest. The Israelites were influenced by these customs and only gradually accepted the worship of one God.

Worship of a bronze bull such as this one (above) formed part of the Canaanite religion.

This 10th-century B.C. Canaanite cult stand, adorned with snakes and birds, was likely used in the worship of Anat, a goddess of war and love.

Gods and goddesses

The various cultures of the Bible Lands had many different gods and goddesses. Despite nominal monotheism, ordinary Israelites sometimes worshiped different Canaanite gods. They venerated golden calves, for example, associated with the rain god Baal, and wooden cult objects representing the fertility goddess Asherah.

Temple traditions

Temples were probably built as homes for gods and goddesses. Canaanite temples appeared in the Early Bronze Age (c. 3150–2200 B.C.)— those excavated all had a wide room, an open porch, and a court.

In about 960 B.C., King Solomon built a Temple in Jerusalem to house the Ark of the Covenant (right), a box containing the precious tablets inscribed with the Ten Commandments.

Above: This breastplate probably belonged to a high priest. It had 12 stones with the names of the 12 tribes of Israel.

Prestige of the priesthood

During the Exodus, the male descendants of Jacob's son Levi were appointed as priests. The role of high priest, established under King David, was invested with the greatest authority. It was reserved for direct descendants of Zadok, Solomon's high priest.

Below: A temple official donating alms to beggars.

Alms to the poor

During biblical times, there was no official aid for the elderly, the disabled, or the poor. Still, giving to the poor was encouraged as a duty. In Old Testament times, farmers donated a tithe (1/10th) of their harvest to priests, travelers, impoverished widows, and orphans. By New Testament times, people brought alms to the temple and synagogues.

❶ LARGE WATER BASINS
❷ PORCH
❸ TWO LARGE, FREESTANDING PILLARS
❹ MAIN DOORS
❺ MAIN HALL
❻ RAISED PLATFORM
❼ HOLY OF HOLIES

❽ THE INTERIOR OF THE TEMPLE WAS OVERLAID WITH PURE GOLD
❾ PRIESTS
❿ HIGH PRIEST
⓫ TWO WINGED CHERUBIMS
⓬ ARK OF THE COVENANT
⓭ ROOF OF BEAMS AND CEDAR PLANKS

Neighboring nations

The religions of neighboring peoples were particularly influential. The Ammonite cult of Molech, for example, was introduced into Israel in King Solomon's time. Greek gods were also incorporated into religion.

Right: A statue of the Assyrian god Lahmu. In the Assyrian and Babylonian traditions, Lahmu and Lahame were the chief gods.

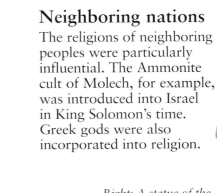

No trace of Solomon's real Temple has ever been discovered. The Bible describes the interior as being 90 feet (27 m) long, 30 feet (9 m) wide, and 45 feet (14 m) high.

Teachers

In Roman times, Jewish education was focused on the Torah (Jewish law) and its traditions. The teacher drilled children to get them to memorize passages from the Torah. Older children, from about 10 upward, learned about the oral Torah, the interpretation of the Torah's commandments. Some teachers livened up these lessons by encouraging students to discuss questions of philosophy and morality.

Writing and Education

The Greek system of education became common throughout the Roman Empire, including Palestine. This relief (above) from a third-century A.D. German tomb shows a teacher with two students. The students are holding scrolls.

Writing first began around 3000 B.C. Trade and administration in the cities of Mesopotamia had become too complex to be recalled by memory alone, and a permanent record of transactions was needed. The first writing is thought to have been Sumerian. It was written in cuneiform, with picture symbols representing words. Education took place primarily in the home, where parents passed on their skills and knowledge to their children, but by Jesus's time, some schools were also available.

Right: Children with their teacher. Lessons often took place in the local synagogue.

Development of writing

Many cuneiform clay tablets from Mesopotamia survive. Written in Sumerian, they are mostly lists of products, laborers, income, and expenses. The Semitic Akkadian language soon followed, using a syllabic system; each sign stood for a syllable. In Canaan around 1500 B.C., the alphabet was invented, which avoided the need for hundreds of symbols for syllables and words. Around 1000 B.C., the Phoenicians improved on the Canaanite alphabet. Hugely influential in the ancient world, Phoenician became the basis for both written Greek and Hebrew.

Right: An example of Phoenician writing. The Phoenician alphabet spread through Syria and what is now Turkey, to Cyprus and the north coast of Africa.

Left: This cuneiform tablet from Mesopotamia indicates how much barley was required to make beer, malt, and other products.

Putting pen to paper

In biblical times, paper was made from papyrus using a technique that had been developed in Egypt around 3000 B.C. Strips of papyrus reed were laid vertically, then others were laid across them horizontally; they were then dried in the sun to form a sheet. Sheets could be pasted together to form a scroll. Pens were made from reeds or rushes sharpened with a knife, and ink from black carbon mixed with oil or gum. People also wrote on wax-coated wooden tablets or pieces of broken pottery.

For long documents, squares of papyrus were pasted together to form a roll. Papyrus was extremely durable—as long as it was kept bone-dry.

Below: These two inkwells probably belonged to scribes. The ink on surviving scrolls from biblical times, such as those discovered near Qumran, is still legible today.

Right: A scribe at work. The profession was open to all who completed specialized training in an advanced school.

Time for school

By the first century B.C., probably under Greek influence, the Jews had set up elementary schools in homes and synagogues. The boys of wealthy families were taught to read and write Hebrew, the language of religion and government. Most ordinary people taught their children at home; boys learned about their faith and the family trade, while girls were taught how to run a Jewish household.

Scribes

Under the Israelite kings, there were professional scribes to record the work of centralized administration, draw up legal documents, record royal decrees, and copy holy writings. They also worked for the public, reading and writing documents for the illiterate. Some scribes also recorded and interpreted the law, a role that gave them great prestige and power.

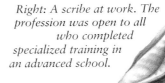

The Bible

A major source of information on the Bible Lands is the Bible itself. It consists of 66 books that were written between 1000 B.C. and A.D. 100—39 in the Old Testament (also known as the Hebrew Bible), and 27 in the New Testament. Jewish people consider only the Old Testament authoritative, while for Christians, the New Testament, which includes the life of Jesus, is the foundation of their religion. The Bible is also sacred to Muslims.

Above: St. Jerome was an Italian scholar (c. A.D. 347–420) who made a Latin translation of the Bible, called the Vulgate, in about A.D. 405.

Writing the Bible

The works of the Bible were originally written on separate scrolls of papyrus or leather and sewn into a book. It is generally accepted that they were written by many different authors, including historians, poets, and prophets. The Old Testament was written mostly in Hebrew and translated into Greek in Hellenistic times. The New Testament was probably written in Greek.

The Old Testament

The Old Testament contains the Jewish holy scriptures. The first five books form the Torah, the holiest section, consisting of Jewish law and history from Creation to Moses's death. Making up the larger part of the Bible, many of the books of the Old Testament tell the stories of prophets such as Isaiah and Daniel.

Right: Israelites crossing the Red Sea between the parted waves, from a 14th-century A.D. Haggadah, a re-telling of the story of the Exodus from Egypt. Exodus is the second book of the Old Testament.

The New Testament

The Christian Bible consists of both the Old and New Testaments. The New Testament contains the four books of the Gospels (Matthew, Mark, Luke, and John), which cover the life and teachings of Jesus. The book of Acts, meanwhile, covers the story from Jesus's Resurrection to the end of the apostle Paul's career. Its later books follow the development of the early Church (see pages 44–45).

Right: This miniature from the Lindisfarne codex, a seventh-century version of the Bible made in Ireland, shows St. Mark writing his Gospel.

People of the Bible

The Bible contains stories of many people, some of whom we know existed in real life; others were probably only legendary characters. In the Old Testament, Moses led the Jewish people out of slavery in Egypt, while King David was the second king of Israel, who expanded Israel's territory and conquered Jerusalem. Jesus's life and teachings are recounted in the New Testament, as are the lives of his disciples, who worked tirelessly to spread Christianity.

Left: Moses holding up the tablets with the Ten Commandments. The story of how he led the Israelites out of slavery is one of the most significant events recounted in the Old Testament.

Right: Some of the jars in which the parchment scrolls were stored.

The Dead Sea Scrolls

The oldest known manuscripts of the Bible were discovered accidentally at Qumran, near the Dead Sea, in 1947. The scrolls, which had been stored in earthenware jars, were incomplete, but probably originally contained all the books of the Old Testament. Many scholars believe the scrolls had been hidden around A.D. 70 by a monastic Jewish sect called the Essenes, who lived in Qumran, in an attempt to protect them from seizure by the Romans during the first Jewish revolt.

Right: Part of one of the Qumran scrolls, which although generally well-preserved, had been damaged by insects and vermin.

Members of the Essene sect hide ancient biblical documents and writings about the Qumran community in pottery jars inside a cave.

Trade and Industry

The commercial importance of the Bible Lands lay mainly in their strategic location between the lands of the East—which exported items such as spices, gold, incense, and ivory—and the market for these goods in the West. Ancient Israel imported many goods and exported agricultural products such as grain, oil, and wine. Goods were transported overland by caravan or shipped by sea. In Old Testament times, industries such as metalworking and clothes-making developed, leading to an expansion in the international trade of raw materials.

Left: This Phoenician glass vessel found in Cyprus was probably used to hold incense. Incense was burned in the Jewish temple each day.

Herod the Great, King of Judaea under the Romans (37–04 B.C.), built an artificial harbor at Caesarea (above) in an attempt to compensate for Palestine's poor natural harbors. Constructed between 22 and 9 B.C., it was a gateway for trade between the East and West.

Trading trips

Sea routes enabled the Bible Lands to trade with the western Mediterranean and down the Red Sea to the east coast of Africa. Traders also brought their wares overland from Anatolia, Syria, Egypt, Arabia, and Mesopotamia. In the first century A.D., conditions for trade were vastly improved when Roman rule brought peace and firm government. The Roman road system (see page 33) made travel easier, the army and police forces made it safer, and the navy prevented piracy at sea.

Sea routes
Land routes

Above: This map shows the major trade routes over land and by sea in biblical times.

Phoenician sailors

Up until Roman times, the Phoenicians controlled sea transport. Their vast trade network stretched along the north African coast to Spain and to the western Mediterranean islands. They established colonies for trading purposes; these included Malta, Sicily, Sardinia, Spain, and Carthage. The Phoenicians exported goods such as cedar wood, glass, and dyed cloth, and purchased silver, tin, and copper.

A variety of materials, including metal weights, were used as currency before coins were invented. Buyers and sellers carried their own weights, like this one (above) in the form of a lion, to ensure that they were not being cheated.

Money, weights, and measures

Before coins were introduced to the Bible Lands around 500 B.C., people either exchanged goods using a barter system or paid for them with an agreed weight of gold or silver. The "shekels" mentioned in the Old Testament were weights rather than coins, and merchants had scales for weighing them.

Right: A Roman coin with an image of the emperor of the time, Vespasian (emperor A.D. 69–79).

Camel caravans

Merchants usually traveled in organized groups called caravans. From the 11th century B.C., camels were used as the beasts of burden. The trek was made in stages. Each caravan went through one area of territory and then transferred the goods to another caravan. Merchants and their camels could rest at a caravanserai, or inn, (see pages 32–33), the majority of which were built along the major overland trade routes.

Right: Camel caravans were a common sight in the Bible Lands. Camels could travel more than 20 miles (32 km) a day.

Crafts and industry

The people of the Bible Lands were skilled craftsmen. There were highly accomplished weavers, carpenters, potters, metalworkers, glassworkers, and jewelers. Many depended on raw materials supplied by traders and sold their finished products to merchants. Linen was imported from Egypt for making clothes. Metals and ores were imported from many different lands, including copper from Cyprus. Luxury goods such as jewelry were created with precious stones imported by Phoenician traders.

An Egyptian figure of a potter making a clay pot on a wheel, from c. 2500 B.C. By the time of King Saul, the first king of Israel (reigned c. 1021–00 B.C.), potters were specialized craftsmen, shaping objects on a turntable rotated with their hand or foot.

Transportation and Travel

Both the Old and New Testaments include many descriptions of journeys, including Abraham's move to Canaan and Jesus's journeys as a preacher. Although the majority of people did not set foot outside their own community, there were many who traveled for migration, trade, or military purposes. Most people traveled on foot or on a humble pack animal; only the wealthy could afford the relative luxury of a cart or chariot.

Donkeys were ridden and used as beasts of burden by those who could afford them.

Resting

Caravanserai grew up along many trade and transportation routes in the Bible Lands. They were large complexes with chambers where traders could sleep and had courtyards for feeding and stabling animals. Water was available from a central well, but people brought their own food. Poor travelers probably slept in the courtyard with the animals, while the wealthier could rent one of the upstairs rooms.

Riding

In Old Testament times, even kings rode donkeys and mules. From 1000 B.C., as international trade developed, camels were increasingly used for transportation. In towns, wealthy people were often carried by servants on litters—curtained couches resting on poles. Only a few people rode horses, which were expensive and, without proper saddles, uncomfortable to ride.

❶ STONE WALL
❷ MERCHANT AND CAMEL
❸ OPEN COURTYARD
❹ ARCADE
❺ ANIMAL STABLES
❻ STONE STAIRCASE
❼ ROOMS
❽ BLANKETS OR MATS TO BLOCK OUT THE SUN

Right: This pottery model from Hamman, Syria, shows a wagon of the type used for transporting goods around 2500 B.C.

Early vehicles

There was little wheeled transportation in Old Testament times. Horse-drawn chariots were used by armies and the wealthy, and wooden carts drawn by donkeys, cattle, or oxen were used on farms. By New Testament times, however, the Romans had built excellent roads, and different types of chariots were used—light, two-wheeled passenger vehicles, and four-wheeled wagons—for transporting goods. They were pulled by horses or mules, or in the case of wagons, sometimes by oxen.

Roman roads

In Old Testament times, roads were merely pathways cleared of obstructions. In Jesus's time, the Romans built a network of paved, durable roads, overcoming many natural obstacles. They built bridges over rivers and tunneled through rock, for example. Built for the convenience of the Roman army, the roads provided invaluable transportation links for local traders as well.

Above: This cross-section of a Roman road shows how it was built. The base is made level with a layer of sand or lime mortar, followed by a layer of lime concrete and broken stone, a third layer of concrete made with gravel, and a top layer formed of stone blocks set in concrete.

Left: This Roman coin from the time of Emperor Augustus (63 B.C.–A.D. 14) shows a carpentum, a two-wheeled cart used as a passenger vehicle by wealthy people.

Out to sea

The greatest seafaring nations in biblical times were the Egyptians and the Phoenicians, who built both warships and merchant ships. The Israelites were not a naval people, although with the assistance of King Hiram of Phoenicia (reigned 969–36 B.C.), King Solomon did succeed in constructing a merchant fleet. In Jesus's time, large freight ships up to 200 feet (60 m) long were seen in the waters around the Bible Lands transporting grain and other goods to faraway lands.

This Roman relief (above) shows a ship buffeted by a storm. Most ships in the Middle East did not set sail between mid-November and mid-March because of the dangerous weather conditions in the Mediterranean.

King David's city

Around 1000 B.C., King David, founder of the joint kingdom of Israel and Judah, captured Jerusalem and made it his capital. He enlarged the city, strengthened its fortifications, and made it the seat of government. King David also installed the Jews' sacred Ark of the Covenant (see page 24) in Jerusalem, giving the city great spiritual significance.

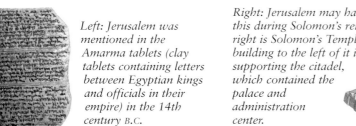

Above: Jerusalem at the time of David probably looked like this.

Left: Jerusalem was mentioned in the Amarma tablets (clay tablets containing letters between Egyptian kings and officials in their empire) in the 14th century B.C.

The city under Solomon

King Solomon recruited forced labor to undertake large public building projects in Jerusalem, doubling the area of the city. The new areas were used for monumental buildings. Solomon constructed a magnificent Jewish Temple in Jerusalem (see pages 24–25), a project that took seven years. For the following six years, laborers worked on the royal palace adjoining it.

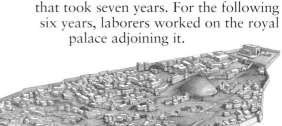

Right: Jerusalem may have looked like this during Solomon's reign. At the far right is Solomon's Temple; the rounded building to the left of it is the wall supporting the citadel, which contained the palace and administration center.

Under the Greeks and Romans

Greek emperor Alexander the Great (356–323 B.C.) conquered Jerusalem in 332 B.C. In 168 B.C., the Seleucid rulers tried to prevent the Jews from observing their customs, but a successful Jewish revolt freed the city of their rule in 164 B.C. In 63 B.C., however, the Romans defeated Jerusalem, and King Herod undertook major building projects. The city became larger than ever.

Left: This glass measuring cup from Jerusalem dates from the first century A.D. Glassmaking became an important industry in Jerusalem and other towns of the eastern Mediterranean at this time.

Below: To placate the Jews, Herod reconstructed the Temple in Jerusalem (work began in 19 B.C.). It took 10 years to complete, and the decoration took a further 74!

Worries over water

The only reliable water source for Jerusalem was the Gihon spring in the nearby Kidron valley. Three underground tunnels to the spring were built between the 10th and 6th centuries B.C. At least one water system was probably installed in King Solomon's time, and one tunnel (which still exists) was constructed under King Hezekiah (reigned 727–698 B.C.). Under siege, the underground tunnels proved invaluable.

Women walked down to the underground tunnels to collect water several times a day. They filled clay water jars, which they balanced on their heads.

Jerusalem

Jerusalem, built high on the hills of ancient Israel, had a turbulent history in biblical times. A place of symbolic importance, King David made it the capital of his united monarchy, and King Solomon built the First Temple there. The Temple was destroyed by the Babylonian king Nebuchadnezzar (reigned 601–561 B.C.) in 586 B.C., and the Jews were exiled; they were allowed to return in 538 B.C. Jerusalem was later conquered by the Greeks and Romans.

Passover was the most popular pilgrimage. People arrived from all over the land. The four roads into Jerusalem were packed with travelers, mostly on foot and carrying all their provisions.

Pilgrimage to Jerusalem

Jerusalem's Second Temple was completed in c. 515 B.C. and helped the city once again become a spiritual center for Judaism. At Passover, Shavuot, and Sukkot, thousands of Jews came to the Temple bringing offerings. Lambs were probably brought for sacrifice at Passover. In Jesus's time, pilgrims outnumbered the normal population of 40,000 by as much as threefold.

Roman soldiers announcing a census. Jewish people particularly resented the periodic censuses, which were used as a basis for taxation. It was also a sign that their lives were controlled by the Roman emperor.

Greek and Roman Times

Both the Greek and Roman Empires had a huge influence on the Bible Lands. When Alexander the Great conquered Palestine and Egypt in 332 B.C., he incorporated them into the vast Greek Empire. When he died in 323 B.C., various Greek-speaking rulers took over much of the ancient world. This was known as the Hellenistic Age. Less than three centuries later, the Romans intervened to settle a civil war in Palestine, and the Roman general Pompey took Jerusalem in 63 B.C. After this, Palestine was ruled by procurators who answered to the Roman emperor.

Above: A Roman charioteer drives his team of four horses forward in a chariot race, an extremely dangerous sport.

The role of religion

The Greek religion spread throughout the Bible Lands under Hellenistic rule. The Greeks worshiped a variety of gods and goddesses, and there was continual pressure on the Jews to assimilate into Greek culture. Some succumbed, others adopted Greek values while remaining Jews, and the most devout stuck to their own traditions. The Romans also worshiped a variety of deities, taking many from the Greeks and renaming them.

Left: This statue of the Greek god Poseidon was found in Israel.

Right: This head of the Greek goddess Aphrodite dates from the third century B.C. and was found in Dor in northern Palestine.

This first-century B.C. Roman frieze commemorates King Herod's celebrations when he became King of Judaea. He offered sacrifices to the Roman god Jupiter: a bull, a sheep, and a boar.

Conquerors and invaders

After the death of Alexander the Great, the empire was divided between two of his generals: Ptolemy and Seleucid. Initially, the Bible Lands were under the control of the Ptolemies, but in 198 B.C., the Seleucids gained the territory and attempted to force Hellenization. In protest, the Jewish people mounted the Maccabean Rebellion in 167 B.C., and they established their own kingdom in 143 B.C. This lasted until their defeat by the Romans.

Life under occupation

Under the Greeks and Romans, military camps were established to maintain order in the Bible Lands. Foreign currencies were introduced, and heavy taxes had to be paid to the occupiers. This was bitterly resented.

Below: These Greek sportsmen are taking part in an athletics contest.

Above: Part of a Greek mosaic floor discovered at the ancient Israelite seaport of Dor, showing a masked man from the Greek comic theater. Many people of the Bible Lands enjoyed attending the theater.

Culture and entertainment

Greek culture had a significant influence on both Jewish and non-Jewish culture in the Bible Lands. Greek soon became the language of trade, and many people, especially the wealthy, adopted Greek customs. The Greeks built their own institutions: each town had an agora, an area with shops, banks, and meeting places; a sports stadium; a gymnasium; public baths; a theater; and a temple. The Romans continued many Greek traditions and also enjoyed sports. They built large amphitheaters, where a favorite spectacle was chariot racing.

Clothing and Appearance

Clothing changed little during biblical times. The main differences in dress were between rich and poor people. A poor peasant had one set of woolen or goat's-hair clothes, while a rich person had outfits of various materials for work and leisure, and for the different seasons. Evidence of people's clothing and appearance comes from biblical descriptions as well as from mosaics, statues, and images of the time.

Above: A typical Israelite man, with cloth headgear, leather sandals, and cloth folded into a belt, which could be used to carry personal belongings and money.

Above: A typical dyeing vat. Cloth and thread were dyed at home or by the town dyer. The indigo plant made the color blue, the murex sea-snail made purple, and the kermes insect, found on oak leaves, made red.

Left: This pottery figurine, dating from about 800 B.C., shows a woman bathing in a tiny tub. Under Greek and Roman influence, bathing at home and at public baths became more widespread.

Homespun clothing

Most people in the Bible Lands wore woolen clothes. Sheep's wool was often dyed and then spun and woven in the home using a loom. Camel hair was used to make coarse cloth, and goat's hair was made into rough cloaks for the poor. Linen was produced in Egypt from the flax plant and turned into fine cloth. The Israelites dyed cloth with plants, minerals, and animal substances.

From head to toe

To protect their heads and necks from the searing summer heat, people usually wore a square of cloth on their heads, held in place by a circle of braided wool. Men sometimes wore a cap. The poorest went barefoot, but others wore leather sandals.

Fashion styles

Both men and women wore a wool or linen tunic—a man's was calf-length, while a woman's reached her ankles and was often blue. This sack-like garment was fastened at the waist with a girdle or belt, and both sexes often had a thick woolen cloak. Married women wore veils over their heads and faces when in public, but unmarried women did not.

Oiled and perfumed

People rarely bathed, as water was scarce in the Bible Lands. They did, however, wash their feet regularly to scrub away the dust from the roads. Both men and women used perfume for cosmetic purposes and to hide body odors. Rich people used expensive, imported scents from India and Egypt, while the poor applied homemade floral or herbal extracts.

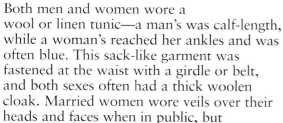

These glass perfume bottles found in Israel date from the first to the third centuries B.C. Imported perfume was a luxury item carefully kept in expensive bottles.

Above: This pair of sandals dates from the second century A.D. People removed their sandals before entering a house or a place of worship.

Pomegranates were grown in the Bible Lands. The ground rind could be used to form a yellow dye.

Hair and makeup

In Old Testament times, Israelites usually had long hair, and men wore beards. Under Greek and Roman rule, men wore their hair short and were clean-shaven. Women often braided or curled their hair. Many wore makeup: black eyeliner and mascara made from ground antimony (a metallic element) were applied to protect the eyes from the sun's glare. Wealthy women used rouge, produced from mulberry juice or red ochre.

Left: This head of a youth with a ribbon in his short, curly hair dates from the period of Greek rule in Palestine.

Right: A cameo of a Roman nobleman. Poor people wore simple items of jewelry usually made from cheap metals such as bronze or iron.

A young woman prepares for her wedding day with the help of her female friends. One has applied makeup from a small stone jar of powder using a bone spatula, and another combs her hair with an ivory comb. The bride wears an embroidered dress and jewelry for her wedding.

In Old Testament times, the Canaanites were skilled jewelers. These gold Canaanite earrings (right) date from the 15th century B.C.

Jewelry

In addition to looking attractive, jewelry was a form of wealth worn by men and women of all classes for special occasions. People wore bracelets, necklaces, anklets, and rings—in their ears and noses as well as on their fingers. These were made from gold, silver, or other metals and set with precious or semi-precious stones.

Invasion and Warfare

The Old Testament is full of examples of warfare and invasion as nations competed for power and different empires took control of the Bible Lands. In the Early Bronze Age (c. 2650–200 B.C.), armies fought with swords, spears, and axes produced from copper and, later, bronze. Warfare became more sophisticated with the development of cavalry and chariots, and the use of siege techniques to conquer cities.

Besieged!

Fortified cities were common in biblical times. Two of the most significant were Megiddo and Masada. When the inhabitants near a city came under attack, they fled there for protection. During a siege, the attackers encircled the fortified city and then attacked it or waited for the inhabitants to be starved into submission. City rulers prepared for sieges by storing food and building water cisterns and underground tunnels leading to water supplies (see pages 15 and 34).

Right: The fortress of Masada. About 1,000 Jews withstood a Roman siege here for three years after the fall of Jerusalem to Rome. When the Romans finally broke the siege, they found that virtually all of the inhabitants had committed suicide rather than submit to the Romans.

The fortress city of Megiddo was one of Solomon's main fortified cities outside Jerusalem. Many battles like this one took place here.

1. A WALL, 12 FEET (3.6 M) THICK, SURROUNDED THE CITY
2. MEGIDDO STOOD NEARLY 70 FEET (21 M) HIGH
3. WARRIORS SHOOT ARROWS FROM THE BATTLEMENTS
4. SIEGEWORKS WERE USED TO BREAK DOWN WALLS
5. ATTACKERS ENCIRCLE THE CITY
6. PEOPLE DEFEND THEMSELVES INSIDE THE CITY WALLS
7. FIRES HAVE BEEN STARTED THROUGHOUT THE CITY

Weapons

A huge variety of weapons were used in biblical times. The Philistines had iron weapons well before the Israelites did. From a distance, opposing armies launched javelins and fired arrows from their bows. Slingshots were also used; Assyrian fighters flung stones from behind their archers. During hand-to-hand fighting, soldiers fought with swords, spears, daggers, heavy clubs, and axes. To protect themselves, they wore body armor and helmets.

Right: These arrowheads were discovered at Masada.

Soldiers and warriors

In early biblical times, armies were composed mostly of foot soldiers. Between 1550 and 1200 B.C., light, two-wheeled chariots were developed by the Egyptians and Assyrians and were introduced into Israel during Solomon's reign. King David established Israel's first professional army, and Solomon added a cavalry. In New Testament times, the Romans had a strong, highly organized army to control their empire.

Right: This warrior from the Middle Bronze Age (c. 2200–1550 B.C.) holds a spear and a "sickle sword" of the type used in Egypt and Canaan.

Above: A scene showing the crucifixion of Jesus. It is written in the Bible that he was killed with two other people, one on either side, and that he died after six hours on the cross—an agonizing death.

Jesus in Jerusalem

In about A.D. 33, Jesus and his disciples went to Jerusalem to celebrate the Jewish Passover. He preached on the Temple Mount and drove traders and money changers from the Temple area. He was angry that the Temple had been turned into a marketplace. Jesus and his disciples ate a final meal together before he was arrested by the Romans, which became known as the Last Supper.

As Jesus rode into Jerusalem on a donkey, the crowds waved palm branches (right) and laid them down in his path.

Crucifixion and resurrection

Jesus was questioned by the Jewish authorities about his actions in the Temple and his claim that he was the Son of God. The Romans tried and convicted him of subverting the nation with this claim, and he was crucified—a brutal form of capital punishment—as a rebel. Christians believe that Jesus was resurrected after this death and appeared to his disciples before ascending to Heaven.

Below: This is a heel bone, pierced by a nail, belonging to a young man who was crucified. Crucifixion victims were often nailed to the cross through the wrists and feet.

Jesus giving his Sermon on the Mount to a large crowd. Jesus explained how people should behave toward one another and how they should serve God instead of devoting their lives to acquiring material goods.

The Life of Jesus

Much of our knowledge of Jesus's life comes from the four Gospels of the New Testament. It is generally agreed that Jesus was born around 6–4 B.C. He grew up in Nazareth, and after being baptized, he began his ministry. According to the Gospels, he preached against injustice, performed miracles, and healed the sick. Jesus's actions, however, angered the Jewish leaders, and he was later crucified as a rebel by the Roman authorities.

Above: It is said that all the inns in Bethlehem were full, so Jesus was born in a humble stable.

Growing up in Galilee

Forced to flee to Egypt because of King Herod's anger at Jesus's birth, Jesus and his family returned to Judaea upon Herod's death. The Bible describes how Jesus grew up in the town of Nazareth in Galilee, northern Palestine. His family was Jewish and followed the customs of their people, which included the annual visit to the Temple in Jerusalem on the festival of Passover (see pages 34–35). Jesus's cousin, John the Baptist, baptized him as a young man.

The Sea of Galilee was a rich source of fish. Jesus's first four disciples— Andrew, Peter, James, and John— were fishermen who left their occupations to join him.

Birth of Jesus

According to the Bible, the forthcoming birth of Jesus was announced to his parents by an angel. He was born just after their arrival in Bethlehem for the census (see page 36). Some days later, three *magi* (astrologers) arrived from the East to pay homage to the baby, bringing precious gifts of gold, incense, and myrrh.

Left: In this illustration from an 11th-century German manuscript, Jesus heals a woman who had been bent over for 18 years. According to the story in Luke's Gospel, Jesus merely laid his hands upon her and she straightened up.

Above: This map shows some of the places that were significant in Jesus's life, including Bethlehem, where he was born; Nazareth, where he grew up; and Jerusalem, where he was put to death.

Teaching and ministry

At about 30 years of age, Jesus began to preach in Galilee. He was based in Capernaum, which was the setting for several of his acts of healing. In Galilee, Jesus recruited 12 disciples, and his popularity increased. Many people saw him as the Messiah, the King of the Jews, who would save the people from the Romans. Great crowds came to hear Jesus's teachings at a meeting in which he instructed people on good conduct; this became known as the Sermon on the Mount (left).

ATLANTIC OCEAN

Lyons

Rome

Smyrna

Edessa

Hierapolis

MEDITERRANEAN SEA

Caesarea

Jerusalem

Alexandria

Above: This map shows the spread of Christianity within 300 years of Jesus's death.

Spreading the faith

In the book of Acts, it is written that there were only 120 believers after Jesus's death. In the ensuing months, Jesus's followers dedicated themselves to spreading his teachings throughout Judaea, Galilee, and Samaria in Palestine. At first, they worked among Jews only, but later, non-Jews were converted as well.

Below: This illuminated manuscript from around 1400 shows Peter and Paul, who played a significant role in the growth of the early Church.

The Apostles

The 12 Apostles had the authority to teach and heal in Jesus's name. The book of Acts focuses on the work of Peter and Paul. Peter was the leader of the early Church for about 30 years. Paul was a Roman citizen who accepted Jesus's message during a religious vision and made three missionary journeys.

Persecuted for their faith

During the first three centuries A.D., Christians were widely persecuted for not following the Roman religion. They suffered torture and execution, and church buildings were destroyed. The first Christian martyr was Stephen; according to the Acts of the Apostles, he was falsely accused of speaking against the laws of Moses and was stoned to death.

Left: Emperor Constantine (A.D. 280–337), who ensured that Christians were no longer persecuted within the Roman Empire.

According to the fourth-century bishop Eusebius, Peter was martyred for his faith by being crucified upside down.

Above: This fifth- or sixth-century eastern Mediterranean vessel was used to hold wine for the Eucharist ceremony, during which Christians share wine and bread.

The first churches

The word "church" initially applied to the worshipers rather than to a building. During a believers' gathering, the Christians related the Apostles' teachings, held discussions, ate a meal, and prayed. The earliest Christians met in the homes of fellow believers. When they did build churches, they were small and unimposing. However, after A.D. 392, when Christianity became the official religion of the Byzantine Empire, churches began to proliferate.

Early Christianity

According to the Acts of the Apostles, the Christian Church was born at Pentecost, 50 days after Jesus's death. Gathered together, Jesus's close companions experienced a powerful religious message, which gave them the courage to spread his word around the world. This was a difficult and dangerous task—early Christians were persecuted by the Romans, and many Jews were suspicious of them. Nevertheless, the centuries following Jesus's death saw the spread of Christianity worldwide.

The early Christians found ways of communicating with fellow Christians through signs. This stone has the words "Our Father" carved into it in a hidden form.

The early Christian community

After Jesus's death, the early believers gathered at Pentecost, and Peter preached the first Christian sermon. It is written in Acts that 3,000 people were converted on that very day. The first Christians continued to worship in the Jewish Temple in Jerusalem, and elsewhere they attended their local synagogues. They also met regularly in each other's homes to discuss their faith. After a while, they realized they needed their own institutions, and churches were established.

Below: This third-century A.D. carving from a Christian coffin shows a group of Christians eating together. Sharing bread and wine in remembrance of Jesus's Last Supper later became known as the Eucharist ceremony.

Early Christians often had to meet in secret and sometimes met in catacombs (above)—underground burial places—to avoid detection.

Index